Jazz Chants®

Rhythms of American English
for Students of English
as a Second Language

CAROLYN GRAHAM

OXFORD UNIVERSITY PRESS

Oxford University Press

200 Madison Avenue
New York, N.Y. 10016 USA

Walton Street
Oxford OX2 6DP England

OXFORD is a trademark of Oxford University Press.

Library of Congress Cataloging in Publication Data

Graham, Carolyn.
Jazz chants.

1. English language—Study and teaching—Foreign students.
2. English language—Spoken English. 3. Music in education.   I. Title.
PE 1128.A2G68   428'.3'4   78-785
ISBN 0-19-502407-9

Printing (last digit): 20 19 18

Printed in the United States of America.

Jazz Chants® is a registered trademark of Oxford University Press.

Dedicated to Scott Joplin, Jelly Roll Morton and to my friend and colleague, Professor Robert Rainsbury, whose spirited performances of the Jazz Chants helped bring them to life.

New York City
1978

Acknowledgments

The Author and the English Language Teaching Department gratefully acknowledge the contributions of the following people who provided the choral response for the tape recording of *JAZZ CHANTS*.

James Anderson
Joyce Berry
Marion Britt
Ellen Chodosh
Portia Clark
Max Cubbon
Alice DePace
Sue Ann Dowd
Michael Fetta

Carol Lemonda
Laurie Likoff
Pat Loewe
Janice Lorimer
Jean Shapiro
Gerald Sussman
Robert Tilley
Chet Wargocki
Neal Wheeler

Contents

Chants and Poems:

* Asterisks indicate Poems

What Is a Jazz Chant?

JAZZ CHANTS are the rhythmic expression of Standard American English as it occurs in situational contexts. The Jazz Chants included in this book and recorded on the accompanying tape are designed as a language acquisition tool to develop the student's appreciation of the rhythm and intonation patterns of Spoken American English.

Just as the selection of a particular tempo and beat in jazz may convey powerful and varied emotions, the rhythm, stresses and intonation patterns of the spoken language are essential elements for the expression of feelings and the intent of the speaker. Linking these two dynamic forms has produced an innovative and exciting new approach to language learning.

Although Jazz Chanting's primary purpose is the improvement of speaking and listening comprehension skills, it also works well in reinforcing specific structures used in a situational context. The natural rhythms and humor of the chants are highly motivating and may be used effectively for both classroom practice and individual home study.

Jazz Chanting was developed at the American Language Institute of New York University where it is an integral part of their language learning program. Teachers of English throughout the United States, Mexico, Canada, Australia and Poland have found *JAZZ CHANTS* to be an exciting and valid teaching tool for effective language acquisition.

How a Jazz Chant Works

The student of Jazz Chanting learns to express feelings through stress and intonation, while building a vocabulary appropriate to the familiar rituals of daily life.

The Chants are a reflection of basic human emotions which occur in specific situations such as *pleasure* at seeing a beloved friend after a long absence (*RETURN HOME*), *anger* (*YOU'RE JUST LIKE YOUR MOTHER*), *frustration* over searching for a misplaced object (*IT'S GOT TO BE SOMEWHERE*), *anxiety* over being late (*PANIC ON BEING LATE*), *possessiveness* (*SELFISH*), *feeling homesick* (*RAIN*), *pain* over a minor physical injury (*OUCH! THAT HURTS!*), and a feeling of general *misery* (*MY FEET HURT*).

THE STRUCTURES

The Chants are written in two-part dialogue form, with the exception of *RAIN* and *TALL TREES* which are both purely exercises in sound and rhythm.

The dialogues include three basic forms of conversational exchange:

1. *Question and response.* This includes Information Questions (*PERSONAL QUESTIONS*), Yes/No Questions (*LOVE SONG*), and questions created by the intonation pattern alone (*JOHN BROWN*).
2. *Command and response.* (*WAKE UP! WAKE UP!*)
3. *Response to a provocative statement.* (*EASY SOLUTIONS*)

The material in the Chants includes the most frequently occuring structures of conversational American English and is intended to provide the student with patterns and vocabulary that he can comfortably use in the world outside the classroom.

Each of the Chants and poems is accompanied by a *Structure Note* which indicates the specific structural focus of the material.

THE SOUNDS

The material in the Chants and on the accompanying tape has been developed to give the student the maximum opportunity to practice the sounds of English *within a meaningful context*. In performing the Chants, the students are actually learning to distinguish difficult vowel and consonant contrasts while they are actively engaged in a verbal exchange which can easily be related to their own experience.

The Chants are particularly useful in developing listening comprehension skills. A comparison of the written text and the tape illustrates the striking difference between the written word and spoken American English. The students are being trained to comprehend the language of an *educated native speaker* in natural conversation.

x

American English stretches, shortens, blends and often drops sounds. These subtle features of the language are extremely difficult for a student to comprehend unless his ear has been properly trained. The sound of, "Jeet yet?" is meaningless unless one has acquired the listening comprehension skills necessary to make the connection with, "Did you eat yet?" Another example of the blending of sounds is the future with *be going to,* as in *I'm going to go,* reduced to *I'm gonna go.* Students should be aware that the written word *gonna* would be considered sub-standard English whereas the spoken form is perfectly acceptable in American conversation.

Each of the Chants is marked with a *Focus* which indicates the specific sounds and intonation patterns demonstrated in the chants and suggests extra practice on those sounds which may present particular problems for the student.

THE PRESENTATION

The essential element in presenting a Jazz Chant is the clear, steady beat and rhythm. By setting the dialogue to a beat, we are not *distorting* the line but simply *heightening* the student's awareness of the natural rhythmic patterns present in spoken American English. A student practicing a specific rhythm and intonation pattern within the Chant form should be able to use that same pattern in normal conversation and be readily understood by a native speaker.

The Chants are based on a combination of *repetition* and *learned response.* Initially, the students should repeat the lines of the Chant following the model provided by the teacher and/or the tape. This choral repetition allows the students to experiment with expressing strong feelings and, in some instances, raise their voices to an angry shout, without the natural shyness that would occur when speaking alone in class.

Once the students are familiar with the material, they progress from the simple choral repetition to giving a group response in answer to a question or statement. This introduces an important new element as the class is now engaged in a dialogue with the teacher. This dialogue may then be transformed into a three or four-part exchange.

It is extremely important that the students have a clear understanding of the meaning of the words they are saying and the appropriate situations in which they might occur. Particular attention should be given to pointing out the difference in emotional impact between the polite and rude forms. For example, the contrast between *Please be quiet* and *Shut up!*

IMPROVISATIONS

Many of the Chants lend themselves to role-playing which enables the student to move from the formal structure of the Chant to an informal classroom improvisation, using what he has learned in a situational context.

Chants which are particularly suited to improvisation include *BABY'S SLEEPING, IT'S GOT TO BE SOMEWHERE* and *PERSONAL QUESTIONS*.

BABY'S SLEEPING suggests a situation where one person or group of persons is creating too much noise and meets with polite and eventually angry complaints.

IT'S GOT TO BE SOMEWHERE may be developed as a game where one student loses an object and moves anxiously around the classroom, using such questions as, **Where is it? Do you have it? Have you seen it?** together with appropriate statements such as, **I can't find it, it's gone** etc. The other students offer helpful suggestions while trying to calm him down: **Take it easy, it can't be lost. Where did you put it?** The game ends when the object is found and the appropriate language of relief and pleasure is spoken: **I found it! Oh, thank heavens! I'm so glad** etc.

PERSONAL QUESTIONS works well as an improvisation with one student as the subject and the class as the prompter asking him *personal* questions at random. The student being questioned must try to avoid giving any specific information. For example:
Where did you go last night? Answer: **Out.**
Who were you with? You don't know him.
How much did you pay for that? Too much.
How much do you make? Not enough.

The improvisations not only give a student the opportunity to speak individually but to make *choices of attitude* in his response.

During the role-playing, it is important that the students retain the rhythm and intonation patterns established in the Chant.

Presenting a Jazz Chant Step-by-Step

The following step-by-step plan for presenting a Jazz Chant is intended to suggest one of the many possible ways of using the material and to share some of the methods I use with my classes in Jazz Chanting at New York University. The teacher should feel free to experiment, improvise and adapt the Chants to the needs of the students. In short, if it works, use it.

STEP ONE — The teacher explains the situational context of the Chant. For example, in *BABY'S SLEEPING* we are learning the different ways in which you tell someone to be quiet. In this case we are asking for silence because the baby is sleeping. The teacher should clearly explain any vocabulary items or expressions which might present difficulties, and may wish to discuss the cultural implications of the material.

STEP TWO — The teacher gives the first line of the Chant at normal speed and intonation. The students repeat in unison. This simple choral repetition continues for each line of the Chant. At this stage the teacher may stop at any point to correct pronunciation or intonation patterns. You may wish to repeat each line several times in chorus.

STEP THREE — The teacher establishes a clear, strong beat by counting, clapping, using rhythm sticks or snapping his fingers. The teacher continues to demonstrate the beat and repeats STEP TWO.

STEP FOUR — The class is divided into two equal sections. There is no limit to the number of students in each section. A Jazz Chant can be conducted with two students or two hundred students. The teacher now establishes a clear, steady beat and gives the first line of the Chant, using normal speed and intonation. The *first section* repeats the line. The teacher gives the second line of the Chant. The *second section* repeats the line. This pattern is continued for each line of the Chant, with the teacher's voice providing a model for the repetitions.

STEP FIVE — The Chant is now conducted as a two-part dialogue between the teacher and the class. The teacher establishes a clear, strong beat and gives the first line of the Chant. The class answers in unison with the second line of the Chant. Until the students are thoroughly familiar with the material, they will probably wish to refer to their open text in class. This two-part dialogue between the teacher and the class is clearly illustrated in the accompanying tape. Notice that at this stage the class is no longer divided into two sections but is *responding* to the Teacher as one choral voice, *without* the teacher's model.

STEP SIX   The class is again divided into two equal sections. The Chant is now conducted as a two-part dialogue between the two groups of students *without* the teacher's model. The teacher establishes a clear, strong beat. Responding to the teacher's hand-cue, the *first section* gives the first line of the Chant, answered by the *second section* giving the second line of the Chant. The teacher is no longer providing a model but is serving as a conductor, keeping a solid, unifying beat while bringing in the two sections at the correct time. I would suggest that the students be allowed to work with open texts for reinforcement. The teacher may find it helpful to say the lines along with the individual sections to retain clarity and maintain the tempo.

Presenting the Poems

The poems, like the Jazz Chants, have been written with a focus on sound contrasts and structures of special interest to the student of English as a Second Language.

The poems are centered on a variety of situations designed to provoke classroom discussion. For example, *SALLY SPEAKS SPANISH, BUT NOT VERY WELL* might serve as an introduction to a classroom discussion on language ability with the students describing their own and perhaps other students' language skills.

I usually introduce a poem by reading it aloud or playing it on the tape while the students listen. It is then repeated line by line with the class in choral repetition. The shorter poems are easily memorized and may be assigned to individual students for presentation in class.

You may wish to experiment with assigning one poem to two students who prepare a joint oral presentation, each speaking alternate lines. For example, in *ON A DIET,* the first student would begin with **First she gave up smoking** and the second student would continue with the second line of the poem, **Then she gave up gin.** This pattern is continued for the entire poem.

Students may be asked to prepare a poem for a class poetry reading and on some occasions students have been inspired to write and present their own poems.

Structure Key

Sh! Sh! Baby's Sleeping!

FOCUS

Practice the pronunciation of **Sh, Hush, Please, quiet.**
Listen carefully for the contraction **Baby's** and the *ing* sound in **sleeping.**
Notice the reduction of sound in the pronunciation of the word **did** when it occurs with **you** in **did you.**

STRUCTURE NOTES

This chant provides practice in the *present continuous* **is sleeping** in contrast to the *simple past,* **What did you say? / I said.**

It also illustrates several ways to complain about noise, from the polite, gentle **Sh! Hush! Please be quiet,** to the angry, rude **Shut up!**

PRESENTATION NOTES

I usually introduce this chant by asking the students what they say when someone is making too much noise. I write their answers on the blackboard, including **Sh, Hush, Please be quiet** and **Shut up,** explaining that the reason we are asking for silence is that the baby is sleeping.

Sh! Sh! Baby's Sleeping!

I said, Sh! Sh! Baby's sleeping!
I said, Sh! Sh! Baby's sleeping!

What did you say?
What did you say?

I said, Hush! Hush! Baby's sleeping!
I said, Hush! Hush! Baby's sleeping!

What did you say?
What did you say?

I said, Please be quiet, Baby's sleeping!
I said, Please be quiet, Baby's sleeping!

What did you say?
What did you say?

I said, Shut up! Shut up! Baby's sleeping!
I said, Shut up! Shut up! Baby's sleeping!

WAAAAAAAAAAAAAAAAAA

Not anymore.

NOTES   Big Mouth John Brown

FOCUS

Practice the pronunciation of the contractions **can't, didn't, don't.**
Notice especially the reduction of sound in the pronunciation of the word **did** when it occurs with **you** in **did you.**
Listen carefully to the contrast in the question intonation pattern of **John who? Who? John Brown?** and the response pattern **I saw John, John Brown.**

STRUCTURE NOTES

This chant provides practice in the *simple past tense* irregular verbs **see/saw, say/said** in contrast with the *simple present* statements, **I can't hear you, I don't believe it.**
It offers useful practice in the negative contractions **can't, don't, didn't** and the use of **anything, nothing, not a.**

Notice the use of **who** in the question, **Who did you see?** Although *whom* is used in the formal written form, *who* is more frequently used in spoken English in the United States.

Big Mouth John Brown

Who did you see?
>I saw John.

John who?
>John Brown.

I can't hear you.
>I said John Brown.

I can't hear you.
>I said John Brown.

I can't hear you.
>I said John Brown.
>I said John Brown.
>John Brown.
>John Brown.

What did he say?
>Who?

John Brown.
>John Brown?

Yes, what did he say?
>He didn't say anything.

Nothing?
>Not a word.

I don't believe it.
I don't believe it.
Big Mouth John Brown didn't say a word?
>Not a word.

I don't believe it.
I don't believe it.
Big Mouth John Brown didn't say a word?
>Big Mouth John Brown didn't say a word.

Rain

FOCUS

Practice the *ing* sound of **raining, falling, soaking.**
Listen carefully to the pronunciation of **stars, shoes, sweet, soft, warm, home.**

STRUCTURE NOTES

This chant illustrates the use of the *past continuous,* **It was raining** with the *simple past,* **I got wet, I stayed outside.**
Notice how the *past continuous* is used to *describe the setting* while the *simple past* introduces *action.*

PRESENTATION NOTES

During the last four lines of the Chant, both voices speak together. This chant should echo the sound of a light spring rain. Try increasing the volume and speed until it sounds like a downpour. Then slowly change the mood, by decreasing speed and volume, until you are left with just a few raindrops and finally silence.

Rain

It was raining, raining, raining hard.
It was falling on my head.

     It was falling on the stars.

It was falling on the sun.

     It was falling on my shoes.

I got soaking wet.

     I got soaking wet.

But I stayed outside.

     I stayed outside.

The rain was sweet.

     The rain was warm.

The rain was soft.
It reminded me of home.

It was raining, raining, raining hard.

     It was falling, falling, falling on the stars.

It was raining, raining, raining hard.

     It was falling, falling, falling on the stars.

Soft rain

     Raining, raining

Sweet rain

     Raining, raining

Warm rain

     Raining, raining

Sweet soft   Raining, raining
Warm rain   Raining, raining
Sweet soft   Raining, raining
Warm rain   Raining, raining

Sally Speaks Spanish, . . .

FOCUS Listen to the third person *s* in **speaks** and the *z* sound in the third person ending of **tries**.
Listen carefully to the pronunciation of **not, very well, really, language, first, thought, speaking, trying.**
Practice the contractions **can't, she's.**
Notice that the *h* sound is dropped in **her** as in **heard her.**

STRUCTURE NOTES This poem moves from the *simple present*, **speaks, tries** to the *present continuous*, **she's speaking, trying** and ends with the *simple past*, **heard, thought, was.**

Notice the use of **but** to introduce an opposing idea.

How's His English?

FOCUS Listen to the third person *s* in **speaks**.
Practice the contractions: **can't, isn't, there's.**
Listen carefully to the pronunciation of **wonderful, very well, accent, perfect, really, native, problem.**

STRUCTURE NOTES This poem is written entirely in the *simple present* tense for both positive and negative statements.

Sally Speaks Spanish, But Not Very Well

Sally speaks Spanish, but not very well.
When she tries to speak Spanish,
you really can't tell
what language she's speaking
or trying to speak.
The first time I heard her,
I thought it was Greek.

How's His English?

His English is wonderful,
he speaks very well.
His accent is perfect.
You really can't tell
that he isn't a native
of the U.S.A.
There's only one problem,
he has nothing to say.

It's Got to be Somewhere

FOCUS

Practice the question intonation pattern of
Where is it?
Practice the contractions **can't, it's.**
Listen carefully to the pronunciation of **got, gone, back, think.**

STRUCTURE NOTES

This chant offers practice in the use of **can't, got to, has to, must;** the command forms **Take it easy, Try to remember, Think back;** and the exclamation over good news, **Thank heavens!** Notice the use of **Whew!** to express relief.

Notice that the word **she** in line 4 of this chant refers to the first voice (usually that of the instructor's). It should be changed to **he** when referring to a male.

It's Got to be Somewhere

Where is it? Where is it?
            Where is it? Where is it?
I can't find it!
            She can't find it!
It's got to be here, it's got to be here!
            It has to be here! It must be here!
It's gone! It's gone!
It's gone! It's gone!
            Take it easy! Take it easy!
It has to be here.
It must be here.
            It can't be lost.
            It can't be lost.
It's got to be here.
It's got to be here.
            Try to remember.
            Try to remember.
I can't remember.
            Try to remember.
I can't remember.
            Think back!
I can't think.
            Think back!
I can't think.
            Where did you put it?
            Where did you put it?
I can't remember.
I can't remember.
Oh, here it is, here it is!
Thank heavens!
            Thank heavens!
I found it.
            She found it!
Here it is! Here it is!
Whew!

Tall Trees

FOCUS

Notice the long, stretched-out sound of **tall trees,** contrasted with the thick, shorter sound of **big.** Listen carefully to the pronunciation of **beautiful, coast, trees.**

STRUCTURE NOTES

A chorus of voices opens this chant and continues in unison, providing a steady beat and background for the soloist who enters with, **The coast of California is a beautiful sight.** The solo voice must keep within the beat and rhythm of the chorus, which continues to chant while the soloist speaks. The solo voice may be assigned to one student or a group of students speaking in unison. The entire chant should be repeated at least three times, increasing the volume each time and ending with a very full sound for **Big trees, tall trees, Big, tall trees.**

This chant is particularly effective if one begins with quite a slow beat and, starting very softly and gently, builds the sound until it evokes the giant redwood trees of California.

Tall Trees

CHORUS	SOLO
Tall trees Tall trees Big, tall trees.	
Tall trees Tall trees Big, tall trees.	
Tall trees, tall trees Big, tall trees.	The coast of California is a beautiful sight,
Tall trees, tall trees Big, tall trees.	with the tall trees, tall trees, big, tall trees.
Tall trees, tall trees Big, tall trees.	The coast of California is a beautiful sight,
Tall trees, tall trees Big, tall trees.	with the tall trees, tall trees, big, tall trees.
Big trees, tall trees Big trees, tall trees Big trees, tall trees Big, tall trees.	

Selfish

FOCUS Listen carefully to the *th* sounds of **this, that** and the final *s* in **yours, hers, ours, theirs.**
Notice the long, stretched-out sounds of **mine, own** and the *ch* sound in linking **get your.**
Practice the contractions: **that's, don't, what's.**

STRUCTURE NOTES This chant offers practice in the *possessive pronouns,* **mine, yours, his, hers, ours, theirs** and in the *demonstratives,* **this/that.**
Notice the strong feeling of **your own** when compared to **yours.**
Note the use of the *present continuous,* **Hey, what are you doing?** to indicate *immediate action taking place.*

PRESENTATION NOTES *Variation: Four-Voice Chant and Chorus*
The chorus begins the chant repeating the single word **Mine** and continues in the background as each of the four voices enters.

	CHORUS
	Mine
	Mine
	Mine
	Mine
This is mine!	Mine
That's yours!	Mine
Don't touch mine!	Mine
Get your own!	Mine

Selfish

This is mine!

       That's yours!

Don't touch mine!

       Get your own!

This is mine!

       That's yours!

This is mine!

       That's yours!

This is mine!

       That's yours!
       That's yours!
       That's yours!

Hey, what are you doing?

       What are you doing with that?

That's mine!

Hey, what are you doing?

       What are you doing with that?

That's his!

Hey, what are you doing?

       What are you doing with that?

That's hers!

What's mine is mine.

       What's yours is yours.

What's his is his.

       What's hers is hers.

What's ours is ours.

       What's theirs is theirs.

What Are You Going to Do at Two?

FOCUS

Listen carefully to the reduction of sound in the question, **What are you going to. . . ?**
Practice pronouncing the question words, **What, Where, Who, How, When.**
Listen to the long stretched-out sound of **leave.**
Practice the sounds of **see, say, stay.**

STRUCTURE NOTES

This poem offers practice in the *future tense* with **be going to.**
Notice the use of the preposition *at* in the time expressions, **at two, at three.**

Meet Me in the Morning

FOCUS

Listen carefully to the pronunciation of **meet, morning, noon, September, middle, midnight, evening.**

STRUCTURE NOTES

This poem offers practice in the use of the prepositions **in, at, the middle of** and the definite article.

Notice the use of the future *will* to indicate a promise: **I'll meet you . . .**

What Are You Going to Do at Two?

What are you going to do at two?
What are you going to do?

Where are you going to be at three?
Where are you going to be?

Who are you going to see?
What are you going to say?
How are you going to go?
Where are you going to stay?

What are you going to do?
Who are you going to see?
When are you going to leave?
Where are you going to be?

Meet Me in the Morning

Meet me in the morning.
Meet me at noon.
Meet me in September,
or the middle of June.

Meet me at midnight.
Meet me in the hall.
Meet me in the summer.
Meet me in the fall.

Meet me in the evening.
Meet me at eight.
I'll meet you anytime you want
but please don't be late.

Taking Credit

FOCUS

Practice the contractions **It's, I'm.**
Listen for the final *s* in **yours.**
Listen carefully to the pronunciation of **whose, sure, beautiful, work, awful, of course, certainly, mine, not.**
Notice the question intonation pattern of **It's his?** contrasted with the response intonation of **It's his.**

STRUCTURE
NOTES

This chant offers practice in the *possessive pronouns* **mine, his, yours;** negative statements and questions with **not;** and the use of **certainly** and **of course** for emphasis.

Taking Credit

Whose book is this?

       It's mine.
       It's mine.

Are you sure it's not his?

       No, No, it's mine!

Whose work is this?
This beautiful work!

       It's mine! It's mine!
       It's mine! It's mine!

Whose work is this?
This awful work!

       It's his! It's his!
       It's his! It's his!

Are you sure it's not yours?

       Of course it's not mine!
       It's certainly not mine!
       Not mine, not mine!

Not yours?

       Not mine!

Are you sure?

       I'm sure!

It's his?

       It's his!

Not yours?

       Not mine!

A Bad Day & More Bad Luck

FOCUS

Listen to the *t* sound in the past tense endings of **overslept, missed, slipped, lost, kicked, bought, went, locked.**
Contrast this with the *d* sound in **sprained, skinned, crawled.**
Practice the contractions: **wouldn't, didn't, couldn't.**

STRUCTURE NOTES

A BAD DAY provides practice in irregular past tense verb forms.

A Bad Day

I overslept and missed my train,
slipped on the sidewalk
in the pouring rain,
sprained my ankle,
skinned my knees,
broke my glasses,
lost my keys,
got stuck in the elevator,
it wouldn't go,
kicked it twice and stubbed my toe,
bought a pen that didn't write,
took it back and had a fight,
went home angry,
locked the door,
crawled into bed,
couldn't take any more.

More Bad Luck

The bread was stale,
it was four days old.
The milk was sour.
The coffee was cold.
The butter was rancid.
The steak was tough.
The service was dreadful.
The waiter was rough.
My bill was huge.
His tip was small.
I'm sorry I went to that place at all.

FOCUS

Listen carefully to the pronunciation of **born, from, home, alone.**
Emphasize the long, stretched-out sounds of **tall** and **old.**
Practice the contractions: **I'd, aren't, weren't.**
Notice the reduction of sound in questions starting with, **Did you...?**
Notice the yes/no question intonation pattern in **Did you have a good time?** contrasted with the intonation pattern of the information question, **How old are you?**

STRUCTURE NOTES

This chant offers practice in *information questions* with **Where, How, How much, Why aren't you, Why don't you, Why weren't you** and yes/no questions with **Did you.**

PRESENTATION NOTES

Notice that the *personal* questions in the chant begin with two perfectly acceptable questions, **Where are you from?** and **Where were you born?** but move to increasingly private questions which would be considered rude in the United States unless asked by very close friends or family.

Personal Questions

Where were you born?

       I'd rather not say.

Where are you from?

       I'd rather not say.

How tall are you?
How old are you?
How much do you weigh?

       I'd rather not say.

How much rent do you pay?

       I'd rather not say.

How much do you make?

       I'd rather not say.

Why aren't you married?

       I'd rather not say.

Why don't you have children?

       I'd rather not say.

Where were you last night?
Why weren't you home?
Did you stay out late?
Did you come home alone?
Did you have a good time?
Did you see a good play?
Did you go to a concert?

       I'd rather not say.

Do You Know Mary?

FOCUS

Practice the question intonation patterns: **Do you know Mary? Mary who?** and notice the contrasting response pattern, **Yes, of course I do.** Note that the *h* sound is dropped when we say **know her, and her.** Listen carefully to the pronunciation of **little, brother, mother, father.** Practice the intonation pattern for, **No, I don't, do you?**

STRUCTURE NOTES

This chant offers practice in the *simple present question,* **Do you know. . .?** and the *emphatic short response,* **Yes, of course I do.**

The entire chant may be practiced with negative answers plus tag questions. Example:

> **Do you know Mary?**
> **No, I don't, do you?**

PRESENTATION NOTES

Repeat the chant, substituting students' names and the names of their families.

Do You Know Mary?

Do you know Mary?

    Mary who?

Mary McDonald.

    Of course I do.

Do you know her little brother?

    Yes, of course I do.
    I know her brother, and her mother
    and her father too.

Do you know her older sister?

    Yes, of course I do.
    I know her older sister, Betty
    and her younger sister, Sue.

Do you know her Aunt Esther?

    Yes, of course I do.
    I know her aunts and her uncles
    and her cousins too.

Do you know her husband Bobby?

    Yes, of course I do.
    I know her husband and his brother
    and his father too.

FOCUS

Listen carefully to the pronunciation of **trip, get back, Gee, been, terribly.**
Notice the *t* sound in the past tense ending of **missed.**
Practice the contractions: **don't, won't, it's, I'm.**

STRUCTURE NOTES

This chant offers practice in *command forms* and the will/won't response to commands. Example:

Call me!

I will.

Don't forget!

I won't.

Notice the use of the future *will* to make a promise.

Departure and Return Home

Departure

Have a wonderful trip!
Have a wonderful trip!
Don't forget to call me
when you get back.

Have a wonderful trip!
Have a wonderful trip!
Don't forget to call me
when you get back.

Have a wonderful trip!

    Don't worry, I will.

Have a wonderful trip!

    Don't worry, I will.

Don't forget to call me.

    Don't worry, I won't.

Don't forget to call me.

    Don't worry, I won't.

Return

Gee, it's good to see you.
You look wonderful!

    So do you!

It's been a long time!

    It sure has.

It's been a long time!

    It sure has.

I missed you terribly.

    Me too!

I'm so glad you're back!

    So am I.

NOTES On a Diet

FOCUS

Listen carefully to the pronunciation of **first, gave up, then, thin.**
Listen to the plural *s* in **mornings, skirts, cans.**

STRUCTURE NOTES

This poem offers practice in the *simple past tense* forms **gave up, wanted, were, ate.**

On a Diet

First she gave up smoking.
Then she gave up gin.
Then she gave up chocolate cake.
She wanted to be thin.

Then she gave up breakfast.
Then she gave up lunch.
On lazy Sunday mornings
she even gave up brunch.

No matter what she gave up,
her skirts were very tight.

'Cause she ate twelve cans of tuna fish
for dinner every night.

Twelve Cans of Tuna Fish Rag

FOCUS

Listen carefully to the pronunciation of **twelve, fish, fat.**
Listen for the third person *s* in **eats** and the plural *s* in **cans.**
Practice the contractions: **that's, she's.**
Practice information question intonation as in **How many, What kind, How often.**
Notice that the line **Twelve cans of fish** is transformed into a question through *intonation* alone.

STRUCTURE NOTES

This chant offers practice in forming information questions including, **How many, What kind, How often** and the exclamations **Oh, my Goodness! You're kidding! No wonder!**

Notice the use of **a lot of** and **too much** and the emphatic short response, **It sure is!**

PRESENTATION NOTES

Before starting this chant, read the poem *ON A DIET,* which introduces the story. This chant should be presented in a quick, bright manner similar to the sounds of early American ragtime music.

Twelve Cans of Tuna Fish Rag

Twelve cans! Twelve cans!
Twelve cans of tuna fish.
Twelve cans.

      How many cans?

Twelve, twelve.

      Did you say twelve?

Yes, I said twelve.

      Twelve cans of what?

Twelve cans of fish.

      Twelve cans of fish?

Yes, fish, yes, fish.

      What kind of fish?

Tuna, tuna.

      Twelve cans of tuna fish?

Yes, twelve cans.

      Oh, my goodness!
      No wonder she's fat!
      How often does she eat
      those twelve cans of tuna?
      How often does she eat
      those twelve big cans?

Every night, every night.
She eats twelve cans of tuna fish
every night.

      You're kidding!
      Oh, my goodness!
      No wonder she's fat!

That's a lot of tuna.

      It sure is!

That's a lot of tuna.

      It sure is!

That's too much tuna, if you ask me.

      It sure is! It sure is!

Twelve cans of tuna is a lot of fish
if you ask me, if you ask me.

      It sure is!
      It sure is!

31

Panic on Being Late

FOCUS

Listen carefully to the pronunciation of **what,
is it, going to be, talk, terribly.**
Notice the long sounds of **now** and **time.**
Practice the contractions: **We're, I'm, don't.**

**STRUCTURE
NOTES**

Notice the use of the infinitive in the pattern:

**I don't have time to see you.
I don't have time to talk to you.**

Panic on Being Late

What time is it?
What time is it?

      Hurry up! Hurry up!
      Hurry up! Hurry up!

What time is it?
What time is it?

      Please hurry up!
      We're going to be late!

Oh, I don't have time
to talk to you now.
I'm late, I'm late, I'm terribly late.

      Hurry up! Hurry up!

What time is it?

      Hurry up! Hurry up!

What time is it?

      Hurry up!

What time is it?

      Hurry up!

Ouch! That Hurts

FOCUS

Practice the pronunciation of **Ouch, stubbed, bit, tongue, bumped, slipped, tripped.**
Notice the *d* sound in the past tense ending of **stubbed,** and the *t* sound in the past tense endings of **bumped, slipped, tripped.**
Watch for the *th* sound of **that,** the third person *s* in **hurts** and the plural *s* in **chairs, stairs.**

STRUCTURE NOTES

This chant offers practice in the *past tense* forms **stubbed, bit, got, bumped, tripped, slipped, fell over.**
Notice the use of prepositions in the phrases, **cramp in my foot, bumped into, tripped on, slipped on, fell over.**

Ouch! That Hurts

Ouch!

What's the matter?

I stubbed my toe.

Oh, that hurts, that hurts.
I know that hurts.

Ouch!

What's the matter?

I bit my tongue.

Oh, that hurts, that hurts.
I know that hurts.

Ouch!

What's the matter?

I got a cramp in my foot.

Oh, that hurts, that hurts.
I know that hurts.

Ouch! Ouch!

What's the matter now?

I bumped into the table,
tripped on the stairs,
slipped on the carpet,
fell over the chairs.

Gee! You're clumsy today!

Would You Walk to China . . . ?

FOCUS

Practice the contractions **I'd, can't.**
Notice the *j* sound in combining **would you,** the
ch sound in combining **can't you,** and the *f* sound
in **have to.**
Listen carefully to the pronunciation of **walk,
leave, with, three, free, sweet.**
Listen for the plural *s* in **plants.**

**STRUCTURE
NOTES**

This poem provides practice in the *unreal
conditional,* **Would you walk to China if you
had the time?** and in forming questions with **Why
can't you** answered by **I have to.**
Notice the use of **never** for emphasis.
Study the time expressions using *at:* **at three, at a
quarter to three.**
Notice the use of the expressions **walk out on** and
take care of.

Would You Walk to China If You Had the Time?

Would you walk to China if you had the time?
Would you leave at a quarter to three?
Would you walk to China if you had the time?
Would you walk to China with me?

Of course, I'd walk to China if I had the time.
I'd leave at a quarter to three.
Of course, I'd walk to China tomorrow night,
if I were only free.

Why can't you walk to China tomorrow night?
Why can't you go to China at three?
Why can't you walk out on your sweet sugar cat
and sail to China with me?

Well, I have to stay home and take care of my plants
take care of my darling too,
and I'd never walk out on my sweet sugar cat
and go to China with you.

FOCUS

Listen carefully to the pronunciation of **black, steak, rare, care, fair, over-easy, truth, really.**
Listen for the plural *s* in **eggs.**
Notice the *d* sound in **scrambled, boiled** and the *t* sound in the ending of **poached.**
Practice the question intonation pattern in **How do you like. . . ?**
Practice the contractions **don't, isn't.**

STRUCTURE NOTES

This chant offers practice in the question pattern, **How do you like . . .** , in reference to the preparation of food and drink. Notice the difference in meaning between the questions, **How do you like your eggs?** (asking the person to make a choice—boiled, fried etc.), and **How do you like your job?** (asking for an opinion—I love it, I can't stand it etc.).

Notice the use of the non-commital answer, **I don't care.** The choice is then returned to the person asking the question. Practice using other similar expressions such as: *It doesn't make any difference to me, It doesn't matter, It's all the same to me.*

Major Decisions

How do you like your coffee?
Black! Black!
How do you like your tea?
With lemon, please.
How do you like your steak?
Medium rare.
How do you like your eggs?
I don't care!
Sunny-side up?
I don't care!
Poached on toast?
I don't care!
Scrambled, with bacon?
I don't care!
Over-easy?
I don't care!
Soft-boiled? Hard-boiled?
I don't care!
How about an omelet?
I don't care!
Come on, tell me!
This isn't fair.
I told you the truth.
I really don't care!

NOTES   I Gave It Away

FOCUS

Practice the question intonation patterns of, **You what? Gave it away? Sell it? You wanted to?** Practice the question and response intonation patterns:

> **What did you say?**
> > **I said I gave it away.**
> **Why didn't you sell it?**
> > **I didn't want to.**

Listen for the reduction of sound in, **What did you** and **Why didn't you.**
Listen carefully to the pronunciation of **gave, want, yes, not.**
Practice the contractions: **that's, didn't.**

STRUCTURE NOTES

This chant provides practice in forming *past tense questions* with *why/what:* **Why didn't you. . . ? What did you. . . ?**
Notice the use of the object pronouns **me, him, her, and them.**
Study the past tense irregular verbs **say/said, give/gave.**

Notice that the question, **You what?** expresses surprise in response to a statement. In conversation, the statement would probably be repeated for clarity.

I Gave It Away

I gave it away.

       You what?

I gave it away.

       What did you say?

I said I gave it away.

       Gave it away?

That's what I said.
I said I gave it away.

       Why?

Because I wanted to.

       You wanted to?

Yes, I wanted to.

       Why didn't you sell it?

Sell it?

       Yes, sell it, sell it.
       Why didn't you sell it?

I didn't want to.

       Why not? Why not?

I didn't want to.

       Why not? Why not?

I didn't want to.

       Why didn't you give it to me?

I didn't want to.

       Why didn't you give it to him?

I didn't want to.

       Why didn't you give it to her?

I didn't want to.

       Why didn't you give it to them?

I didn't want to.
I didn't want to.

Banker's Wife's Blues

FOCUS   Practice the pronunciation of the question words,
                   Where, When, Why.
                   Listen carefully for the third person *s* in **lives,
                   works, sleeps, loves** and the *ies* in **studies.**
                   Notice that the *h* sound is dropped in **does he.**

**STRUCTURE   This chant offers practice in *simple present, third
NOTES**   person information questions* and *response.*
                   Note the comparative pattern **more than** and the
                   use of the preposition and article structure: **at the,
                   near the.**

Banker's Wife's Blues

Where does John live?

> He lives near the bank.

Where does he work?

> He works at the bank.

When does he work?

> He works all day
> and he works all night,
> at the bank, at the bank,
> at the great, big bank.

Where does he study?

> He studies at the bank.

Where does he sleep?

> He sleeps at the bank.

Why does he spend all day, all night,
all day, all night,
at the bank, at the bank?

> Because he loves his bank
> more than his wife
> and he loves his money
> more than his life.

Tell Me Your Name

FOCUS

Listen to the long, stretched-out sounds of **name** and **please**.
Practice the pronunciation of **first, last, beautiful, again.**

STRUCTURE NOTES

This poem provides practice in gentle, *polite commands* with **please** and *exclamations* with **What a . . . !**
Notice the use of **again**, and the contrast in the use of **say/tell.**

Sand

FOCUS

Practice the contractions: **I'd, it's.**
Listen carefully to the pronunciation of **feel, felt, beach, back, been.**
Notice the *z* sound in the plural ending of **shoes, clothes, eyes, toes.**
Listen for the *h* sound in **hate, hair.**

STRUCTURE NOTES

This poem provides practice in the *unreal conditional* pattern, **If I were, I would,** and the *present perfect* pattern, **It has been, I have felt.**
Notice the use of the expressions **full of, out of** and the prepositions **in, to,** and **between.**

Tell Me Your Name

Tell me your name again, please.
Tell me your name.

Tell me your first name.
Tell me your last name.

Spell your name for me, please.
Spell your name.

Pronounce your name for me, please.
Say it again.

What a beautiful name!
What a lovely name!

Sand

If I were home,
If I were home,
I'd run to the beach,
take off my shoes
and walk in the sand.

I'd shake the sand out of my shoes.
I'd feel it between my toes.
I'd smell wet sand in my hair.
I'd feel it in my eyes.

My face would sparkle from the sand.
I would say, "I hate this sand."

Back home, the bed would be full of sand
and my clothes, and my hair.
I would wake up and feel the sand in my hair.

Oh, it's been so long
since I have felt sand
in my hair.

Late Again

FOCUS	Listen carefully to the pronunciation of **not quite, just a minute, in a minute.** Practice the contractions: **don't, I'll, can't, let's.** Notice the long, stretched-out sounds of **find, shoes, hand, keys, floor.** Listen for the plural *s* in **keys, socks, shoes.**
STRUCTURE NOTES	Notice the use of the future *will* to indicate a promise: **I'll be ready in a minute.**

Late Again

Are you ready?
Are you ready?
Are you ready to go?

       Not quite, not quite.
       Just a minute, don't rush me!

Hurry up, hurry up!
Hurry up, hurry up!

       I'll be ready in a minute,
       in a minute, in a minute.
       I can't find my keys!
       I can't find my keys!

Come on, let's go!
Come on, let's go!

       I can't find my socks!
       I can't find my socks!

Come on, let's go!
Let's go, let's go!

       I can't find my shoes!
       I can't find my shoes!

Come on, let's go!
Let's go, let's go!

Your keys are in your hand.
Your socks are in your shoes.
Your shoes are on the floor.
Let's go, let's go!

NOTES   # Warning

FOCUS

Listen carefully to the pronunciation of **out, hole, huge, think, house, believe.**
Practice the *ch* sound in **watch** and the *ing* sound in **teasing, kidding.**
Practice the contractions: **there's, don't, it's, you're.**
Notice the one-word question intonation patterns: **What? Where? Big? Huge?**

STRUCTURE NOTES

This chant offers practice in the *command pattern,* **Watch out!** and the *negative statements,* **I don't see any, There's no hole.**

Notice the use of the preposition and definite article **in the** and the comparative form, **big as a house.**

Warning

Watch out! Watch out!
Watch out! Watch out!
Watch out!
There's a hole in the floor!

      What?

A hole.

      Where?

In the floor.

      A hole in the floor?

Yes, a hole in the floor,
A great big hole in the floor.

      Well, I don't see
      any hole in the floor.
      I don't see any hole.

It's there!

      Where?

Right there!

      Right here?

Yes, right there.

      Are you sure?

Sure, I'm sure.
It's big as a house.

      Big?

It's huge.

      Huge?

It's huge.
A huge hole, a great big hole,
a great big hole in the floor.

      I think you're kidding.
      You're teasing me.
      There's no hole in the . . .

FOCUS

Practice the *teen* sounds in **fourteen** and **thirteen**.
Listen carefully to the pronunciation of **pretty good**.
Notice the long, stretched out sounds in **long, old, known, mine**.
Listen to the *th* opening sound in **thirteen** and the *th* ending in **both**.
Practice the contractions: **I've, he's, we're, they're**.

STRUCTURE NOTES

This chant offers practice in the *present perfect question and response* pattern: **How long have you known / I've known . . . for . . . .**
It also illustrates the use of the indefinite article *a/an* in **a dear, an old friend**.

PRESENTATION NOTES

Notice that the refrain, **She's known Jack for fourteen years. / He's a pretty good friend of hers,** refers to a female first speaker. If the first speaker is a male, the line should be changed to read:

He's known Jack for fourteen years.
He's a pretty good friend of his.

Friends

Well, I've known Jack for fourteen years.
He's a pretty good friend of mine.

> She's known Jack for fourteen years.
> He's a pretty good friend of hers.

And I've known Bill for thirteen years.
He's a pretty good friend of mine.

> She's known Bill for thirteen years.
> He's a pretty good friend of hers.

I've known them both for quite a long time.
They're pretty good friends of mine.

> She's known them both for quite a long time.
> They're pretty good friends of hers.

I've known Jim for a long time.
He's an old, old friend of mine.

> She's known Jim for a long time
> He's an old, old friend of hers.

We're old friends, old friends.
He's a dear, old friend of mine.

> How long have you known your old friend Sue?
> How long have you known dear Claude and Sue?

Well, I met them just before I met you.
They're my closest friends, dear Claude and Sue.

Easy Solutions

FOCUS

Listen carefully to the pronunciation of **sandwich, chilly, itches, scratch, awhile.**
Practice the contrast in sound of **angry/hungry.**
Practice the contractions: **I'm, it's, I've.**
Practice the pronunciation of **Gee!**

STRUCTURE
NOTES

This chant offers practice in giving an appropriate response to a provocative statement; using *simple present tense* to indicate a general condition, **My feet hurt;** and the *command form* in the response, **Sit down for awhile.**

Easy Solutions

Gee, I'm hungry!

      Have a sandwich.

Gee, I'm angry!

      Calm down!

Gee, I'm sleepy!

      Take a nap!

Gee, it's chilly in here!

      Put on a sweater.

Gee, it's hot in here!

      Open a window.

I've got the hiccups!

      Drink some water.

My nose itches.

      Scratch it.

My feet hurt.

      Sit down for awhile.

My shoes are tight.

      Take them off.

I have a toothache.

      Go to the dentist.

I have a headache.

      Take some aspirin.

I'm lonely!

      Call up a friend.

I'm bored!

      Go to a movie.

NOTES   Love Song

FOCUS

Listen carefully to the pronunciation of **love** and **leave.**
Notice the *h* sound is dropped in: **Does he, is he, will he, hug her, kiss her, leave her, hug him, kiss him, leave him, love her, love him.**
Notice the third person *s* in **knows.**
Listen to the rising yes/no question intonation pattern throughout the chant.

STRUCTURE NOTES

This song provides practice in forming questions in the *simple present tense,* using the verb *to be* and other verbs and the *future* with *will*.
It may be used as the basis for a response practice drill, contrasting the verb to be, **Is she happy? Yes, she is** with other verbs, **Does she love him? Yes, she does.**

Love Song

Does she love him?
> Yes, she does.

Is she happy?
> Yes, she is.

Does he know it?
> Yes, he does, yes, he knows it.

Will she hug him?
> Yes, she will.

Will she kiss him?
> Yes, she will.

Will she leave him?
> Yes, she will, if she has to.

Does he love her?
> Yes, he does.

Is he happy?
> Yes, he is.

Does she know it?
> Yes, she does, yes, she knows it.

Will he hug her?
> Yes, he will.

Will he kiss her?
> Yes, he will.

Will he leave her?
> Yes, he will, if he has to.

Are they happy?
> Yes, they are.

Are they lucky?
> Yes, they are.

Do they know it?
> Yes, they do, yes they know it.

Will he find somebody new?
Will she find somebody too?
> Yes, they will.
> Yes, they will, if they have to.

On the Rocks

FOCUS

Listen carefully to the pronunciation of the third person *s* in **listens, talks, sits** and the *es* in **watches.**

STRUCTURE NOTES

This chant provides practice in the *simple present tense* with emphasis on the third person singular.

Notice the use of *never,* as in **He never listens to me,** and contrast this with the *negative form,* **He doesn't listen to me.**

On the Rocks

You never listen to me.

        What did you say?

You never listen to me.

        What?

He never listens to me.
He never talks to me.
He just sits around,
and watches TV.

        She never listens to me.
        She never talks to me.
        She just sits around,
        and watches TV.

She never listens to me.

        She just sits around.

She never talks to me.

        She just sits around.

She just sits around.

        She just sits around,
and watches TV.

        She just sits around.

He never listens to me.

        He just sits around.

He never talks to me.

        He just sits around.

He just sits around.

        He just sits around,
and watches TV.

        He just sits around.

The Beaches of Mexico

FOCUS

Listen carefully to the pronunciation of **seen, been, again.**
Notice the *t* sound in **walked.**
Listen for the plural ending in **beaches** and **streets.**

STRUCTURE NOTES

This poem provides practice in the *present perfect* pattern, **Have you ever been** and the response, **I've been / I've never been.**
Notice the use of *sure* for emphasis in, **I've sure been.**

The Beaches of Mexico

Have you ever seen the beaches of Mexico?
Have you ever walked the streets of San Juan?
Have you ever been to Haiti?
Have you ever been to Spain?
Have you ever walked barefoot
in a heavy rain?

Have you ever been in trouble?
Have you ever been in pain?
Have you ever been in love?
Would you do it all again?

Well, I've never seen the beaches of Mexico.
I've never walked the streets of San Juan.
I've never been to Haiti.
I've never been to Spain.
I've never walked barefoot
in a heavy rain.
But I've sure been in trouble,
I've sure been in pain,
I've sure been in love,
I'd do it all again.

I'm Sorry, But...

FOCUS   Listen carefully to the pronunciation of **You've got to.**
Practice the contractions: **I'm, you've, it's, can't, won't, I'll, don't.**
Listen to the *ing* endings of **doing, walking, working.**
Practice the pronunciation of **walk, work, can, can't.**

**STRUCTURE
NOTES**   This chant provides practice in the use of the *modal auxiliary*, **have got to,** to express necessity. It also illustrates the *comparative forms*, **as hard as, harder, as fast as, faster** and the irregular *comparative/superlative* forms **better, best.**

I'm Sorry, But...

I'm sorry, but you've got to do better than this.
      I'm doing the best I can.
I'm sorry, but you've got to walk faster than this.
      I'm walking as fast as I can.
I'm sorry, but you've got to work harder than this.
      I'm working as hard as I can.

It's not good enough
It's not good enough
It's not good enough
It's not good enough

      I'm doing my best.
Try a little harder.
      I'm doing my best.
Try a little harder.
      I'm doing my best.
Try a little harder.
      I can't, I can't.
Don't say can't.
      I won't, I won't
      but I'm doing my best.
Do a little better.
      I'm doing my best.
Do a little better.
      I'm doing my best.
Try a little harder.
      I'll try, I'll try.
Try a little harder.
      I'll try, I'll try.

Baby Bobby

FOCUS

Listen carefully to the pronunciation of **bought, bright, blue, blanket, baby, boy, bad, very, angry.**
Listen for the third person *s* in **hates, drives** and the *th* sound of **that.**
Practice the contractions: **mother's, father's.**
Listen for the plural endings in **glasses, keys, buttons.**
Notice the reducation of sound in, **Why did you do that?**

STRUCTURE NOTES

This chant provides practice in the *irregular past tense* forms: **bought, cried, broke, lost, threw, cut, got.**

Notice the use of the *simple present tense* to describe a permanent condition: **He hates bright blue. He drives everybody crazy.**

Baby Bobby

Betty bought a bright blue blanket
for her baby boy.
He cried when he saw it.
He hates bright blue.

Betty bought a blanket.
      Betty bought a blanket.
Betty bought a blue blanket.
      Betty bought a blue blanket.
Betty bought a bright blue blanket
      a bright, blue blanket
for her baby boy.
      for her baby boy.
He cried when he saw it.
      He hates bright blue.

Betty's baby's name is Bobby.
      Baby Bobby is a bad, bad boy.
Bobby is a bad, bad baby.
      He drives everybody crazy.
Bobby is a bad, bad baby.
      Baby Bobby is a bad, bad boy.
Bobby broke his mother's glasses.
      Bobby Baby! Why did you do that?
Bobby lost his father's keys.
      Bobby Baby! Why did you do that?
Bobby threw the paper in the kitchen sink.
      Daddy got very, very angry.
He cut all the buttons off his father's shirt.
      Daddy got very, very angry.
Bobby is a bad, bad baby.
      Baby Bobby is a bad, bad boy.

It's Like Winter Today

FOCUS   Practice the contraction **it's**.
                   Listen for the third person *s* in **looks, feels** and
                   the final *z* sound in **close**.
                   Notice the plural *s* ending of **windows**.

STRUCTURE   This poem illustrates the use of **to be like, to**
NOTES   **look like, to feel like.**
                   It includes the command forms: **Close, Shut,**
                   Light, Hold, Open, Turn off.

It's Like Winter Today

It's like winter today.
It looks like winter.
It feels like winter.
Close the windows!
Shut the door!
Light the stove!
Hold me!

It's like spring today!
It looks like spring.
It feels like spring.
Open all the windows!
Open the door!
Turn off the stove!
Hold me!

My Feet Hurt

FOCUS

Listen carefully to the pronunciation of **hurt, hot, here.**
Notice the long, stretched-out sounds of **cold, shoes, gloves.**
Listen for the plural *s* in **hands, gloves, shoes.**
Practice the contraction **It's.**

STRUCTURE NOTES

This chant offers practice in giving an appropriate response to a provocative statement; using *simple present* to indicate a general condition, **It's cold in here;** and the *command response,* **Put on your sweater.**
It also provides practice in the two-word verbs: **take-off, put-on.**

My Feet Hurt

My feet hurt!
>Take off your shoes!

My feet hurt!
>Take off your shoes'

My feet hurt!
>Take off your shoes!

My feet hurt!
>Take off your shoes!

It's hot in here!
>Take off your sweater!

It's hot in here!
>Take off your sweater!

It's hot in here!
>Take off your sweater!

My feet hurt!
>Take off your shoes!

It's cold in here!
>Put on your sweater!

It's cold in here!
>Put on your sweater!

It's cold in here!
>Put on your sweater!

My feet hurt!
>Take off your shoes.

My hands are cold!
>Put on your gloves!

My hands are cold!
>Put on your gloves!

My hands are cold!
>Put on your gloves!

My feet hurt!
>Take off your shoes!

Mama Knows Best

FOCUS   Listen carefully to the pronunciation of **shouldn't, ought to, this, that, them, hat, hair, fat, pear.**

STRUCTURE NOTES   This poem provides practice in the use of the *modal auxiliaries,* **shouldn't, ought to,** when giving advice.
Notice the use of the demonstratives: **this, that.**

Mama Knows Best

You shouldn't do it that way.
You ought to do it this way.

    You ought to do it this way.
    You ought to do it my way.

You shouldn't wear it that way.
You ought to wear it this way.

    You ought to wear it this way.
    You ought to wear it my way.

You shouldn't go with them.

    You ought to go with us.

You shouldn't take the train.

    You ought to take the bus.

You shouldn't wear that hat.

    You ought to cut your hair.

You shouldn't get so fat.

    You ought to eat a pear.

You shouldn't do it that way.

    You ought to do it this way.
    You ought to do it this way.

You ought to do it my way.

FOCUS

Listen to the third person *s* in **gets, wakes, sleeps.**
Notice the third person plural form in, **His cats get up.**
Listen carefully to the pronunciation of **wish, find, four, fat, flies, flew, Friday, not.**

STRUCTURE NOTES

These poems move from the *simple present tense,* **Fred gets up,** to the *simple past,* **Fred gave a party.**
The third poem introduces the use of **I wish I could.**
Practice the *irregular past tense* forms: **gave, came, left, went, had to, flew.**
Notice the use of the prepositions: **in, on, in my window, on me.**

The Fred Poems

Fred Gets Up at Eight O'Clock

Fred gets up at eight o'clock,
his cats get up at seven.
His dog wakes up at ten to six,
but his bird sleeps 'till eleven.

Fred Gave a Party But Nobody Came

Fred gave a party, but nobody came.
Nobody came but his Mom.
Fred gave a party, but nobody came.
Nobody came but Tom.
Tom left early.
Mom went home.
Fred had to stay at his party
alone.

Four Fat Flies

I wish I could find
those four fat flies
that flew in my window
last Friday night.

Four flies flew in,
four flies, not three.
One landed on Fred,
three landed on me.

NOTES   Big Bill Bell

FOCUS

Practice the contractions: **he's, who's, Bill's, that's.**
Notice the *h* sound is dropped in **know him.**
Practice the contrasting sounds of **big, Bill, Bell.**
Listen carefully to the pronunciation of **very well.**
Notice the question intonation pattern of: **Who's here? Bill who? Who's he? I do? He is?**
Notice the final *s* in **yours.**

STRUCTURE NOTES

This chant provides practice in the use of the *subject/object* pronouns **he/him.**

Big Bill Bell

He's here!

       Who's here?

Bill's here.

       Bill who?

Bill Bell.

       Bill Bell? Who's he?

You know him.

       I do?

Of course you do.
He's a friend of yours.

       He is?

Of course he is.
Big Bill. Big Bill Bell.

       Oh, you mean Bill!
       Big Bill!

That's right, that's him!
You know him very well.

       Sure I do!
       Big Bill Bell!
       Big Bill Bell!
       I know him very well.

Wake Up! Wake Up!

FOCUS

Listen carefully to the pronunciation of **I don't want to** and **You're going to be.**
Practice the pronunciation of **wake up, get up, come on, late, work.**
Notice the pronunciation of **have to, you've got to.**

STRUCTURE NOTES

This chant provides practice in the *command forms,* **Wake up! Get up!** and the use of **Come on** for added emphasis.
It also illustrates the use of the *modal auxiliaries,* **have to, must, have got to** and the future with **be going to.**

Wake Up! Wake Up!

Wake up! Wake up!
>What time is it?
Wake up! Wake up!
>What time is it?
It's time to get up.
>What time is it?
It's time to get up.
>What time is it?
Come on, get up!
>I don't want to get up.
Come on, get up!
>I don't want to get up.
You have to get up!
>I don't want to get up.
You must get up!
>I don't want to get up.
You've got to get up!
>I don't want to get up.
Come on, get up!
>I don't want to get up.
Get up! Get up!
You're going to be late!
>Late for what?
Late for work.
>Late for work?
>It's Sunday!

Well, He Eats Like a Pig

FOCUS

Listen for the third person *s* ending in: **eats, works, looks, smokes, sleeps, drinks, gets, talks.**
Notice the *z* sound in the ending of **cries.**
Watch for the plural *s* in **packs.**
Practice the contractions: **can't, he's, I've.**

STRUCTURE NOTES

This poem provides practice in the *simple present tense,* third person singular.
The final line is a very useful pattern of American English speech, the *superlative* followed by the *present perfect,* as in **the dearest friend I've ever had.**

Notice the use of *hardly* in **he hardly talks,** meaning *almost never, seldom* or *rarely.*

Well, He Eats Like a Pig

Well, he eats like a pig,
he can't get enough.
He works like a dog,
he looks real tough.
He smokes like a chimney,
four packs a day.
He sleeps like a log,
what more can I say?

He drinks like a fish,
scotch on the rocks.
When he gets real mad,
he hardly talks.
He cries like a baby
when he's feeling sad.
He's the dearest friend
I've ever had.

You're Just Like Your Mother

FOCUS

Listen to the question intonation pattern in **Stop what?**
Practice the pronunciation of **stop, arguing, not, argue.**
Practice the contractions: **I'm, you're, don't, doesn't.**
Notice the sharp contrast in rhythm and intonation pattern of *Yes, you* **are**/*No, I'm* **not** and the more emphatic *You* **are** *too*/*I* **am** *not*.

STRUCTURE NOTES

This chant provides practice in the short response (positive, negative) moving from the verb **to be** to other verbs: **Yes, you are, No, I'm not, Yes, she does, No, she doesn't.**

You're Just Like Your Mother

Stop it!

       Stop what?

Stop arguing with me.

       I'm not arguing with you.

Yes, you are.

       No, I'm not.

Yes, you are.

       No, I'm not.

You are too!

       I am not!

You are too!

       I am not!

You're just like your mother.

       I am not!

Yes, you are!

       No, I'm not!

Yes, you are!

       No, I'm not!

She loves to argue.

       No, she doesn't!

Yes, she does!

       No, she doesn't!

Yes, she does!

       No, she doesn't!

She does too!

       She does not!

She does too!

       She does not!

Don't argue with me!

About the Author

Carolyn Graham, a graduate of the University of California, Berkeley, settled in Turkey for nine years where she taught English as a Second Language in Ankara and Istanbul. After one year of study in Paris, she returned to the United States in 1969, and joined the faculty of the American Language Institute, New York University. She has presented workshops in Jazz Chanting in England, Canada, Mexico and major cities throughout the United States.

She is also a professional entertainer, playing ragtime piano and jazz kazoo in various clubs in New York City, under the name of Carolina Shout.